TABLE OF CONTENTS

INTRODUCTION

The Cloze activities were developed to accompany your reading program. These lessons are meant to serve not only as practice for cloze tests, but also as a means of strengthening holistic reading ability. Studies have shown that cloze exercises paired with specific comprehension strategies are valid reading instructional activities.

ORGANIZATION OF BOOK

The book is organized into eleven units that each focuses on one skill. The skills include circling clue words, using what you know, reading and then checking, reading beyond the blank, circling clue words before and after the blank, using a 3- and 5-option process of elimination, using redundant clues, forming categories, finding causes and effects, and using process of elimination. Four assessment tests have been provided for use as a pretest and post-test of skills.

TEACHING TIPS

The following points should be kept in mind when administering the practice activities in this book:

1. Cloze activities should be untimed. When planning to administer an activity or series of activities, allow enough time for all students to complete the assignment comfortably.

2. Since the basic learning objective of a cloze activity is to restore meaning to text, it is essential that students consistently reread their work once closure has been made. Eliminating the final confirmation reading deprives the student of the essential step in the comprehending process.

3. Students should be instructed to go through the following steps whenever practicing the cloze technique:
    a. make preliminary predictions
    b. establish schema
    c. access their prior knowledge
    d. reread to confirm predictions, and
    e. make any necessary changes if previous predictions were modified.

4. The activities use basic thinking and comprehending skills stressed in most reading programs.

5. Practice is given in the modified cloze technique, using five syntactically correct options as in many reading tests.

IMPLEMENTATION

The activities in this book are designed for independent use by students who have had instruction in the specific skills covered in the lessons. Copies of the activity sheets can be given to individuals or pairs of students for completion. When students are familiar with the content of the worksheets, they can be assigned as homework.

To begin, determine the implementation that fits your students' needs and your classroom structure. The following plan suggests a format for this implementation.

1. **Administer** the Assessment Test to establish baseline information on each student. This test may also be used as a post-test when the student has completed a section.

2. **Explain** the purpose of the worksheets to the class.

3. **Review** the mechanics of how you want students to work with the activities. Do you want them to work in pairs? Are the activities for homework?

4. **Introduce** students to the process and purpose of the activities. Work with students when they have difficulty. Give them only a few pages at a time to avoid pressure.

ADDITIONAL NOTES

1. Parent Communication. Send the Letter to Parents home with students.

2. Bulletin Board. Display completed worksheets to show student progress.

3. Curriculum Correlation. This chart indicates curriculum areas incorporated in the activities to help you in your daily lesson planning.

4. Student Progess Chart. Duplicate the sheets found on pages 6-7. Record each student's name at the top. Note the date assigned and the completion of each lesson for each student.

Dear Parent:

During this school year, our class will be working on reading skills. We will be completing activity sheets that provide practice with cloze exercises. These exercises are meant to serve not only as testing practice, but also as a means of strengthening your child's reading ability.

From time to time, I may send home activity sheets. To best help your child, please consider the following suggestions:

- *Provide a quiet place for your child to work.*
- *Go over the directions together.*
- *Encourage your child to do his or her best.*
- *Check the lesson when it is complete.*
- *Go over your child's work, and note improvements as well as problems.*

Help your child maintain a positive attitude about reading. Provide as many opportunities for your child to read as possible. Read books from the library, comics in the newspaper, and even cereal boxes. Let your child know that each lesson provides an opportunity to have fun and to learn. Above all, enjoy this time you spend with your child. He or she will feel your support, and skills will improve with each activity completed.

Thank you for your help!

Cordially,

CURRICULUM CORRELATION

	Unit	**Page**
Art	7, 8, 9	41, 42, 43, 45, 46, 47, 48, 49, 50, 51
Biography	1, 7, 8, 9	10, 11, 41, 42, 43, 46, 47, 48, 49
Science	1, 2, 3, 6, 8, 10	12, 13, 14, 15, 16, 17, 18, 19, 20, 24, 25, 26, 27, 35, 36, 37, 38, 44, 54, 55, 56, 57, 58
Social Studies	1, 2, 3, 6, 8, 10, 11	10, 11, 21, 22, 23, 50, 51, 59, 60, 61, 62
Health	3	26, 27
Math	4, 5	30, 31, 32, 33, 34

Name ______________________ Date ______________________

CLOZE: GRADES 2-3

STUDENT PROGRESS CHART

Skill	Page	Date Assigned	Date Completed	Comments
Circle clue words	10-11			
	12-13			
Use what you know	14			
	15			
	16-17			
	18-20			
	21-22			
Read and then check	23			
	24-25			
	26-27			
Read beyond the blank	30-31			
Circle clue words before and after the blank	32-33			
	34			
3-option process of elimination	35			
	36			
	37			
	38			

Name ______________________________ Date ______________________________

CLOZE: GRADES 2-3

STUDENT PROGRESS CHART

Skill	Page	Date Assigned	Date Completed	Comments
5-option process of elimination	41			
	42-43			
Use redundant clues	44			
	45			
	46-47			
Form categories	48			
	49			
	50-51			
Find causes and effects	54-55			
	56			
	57			
	58			
Process of elimination	59			
	60			
	61			
	62			

Name ______________________ Date ______________________

Assessment: Units 1, 2, 3

Read the following paragraph. Then write two words, or groups of words, that show the underlined word doesn't make sense in the paragraph.

The dogs that help the blind are called Seeing Eye dogs. These dogs must go to special schools where they learn many rabbits. The person who wants the Seeing Eye dog must also go to the same school.

1. ______________________

2. ______________________

Read the following paragraphs. Think about the underlined words. Write a word on the line that makes more sense. Then, read the story over to check the meaning.

A raindrop named Splash slides down the trunk of a tree. It smells on a little plant at the bottom of the tree. Splash slips down a leaf. It goes into a little pool made by many other raindrops.

3. ______________________

Splash sinks into the ground, under little roots, and slides around some rocks. Splash stops. It rests on one of the big tree toys. Then it is pulled inside the root. Pop! Slowly Splash goes up the root. Then Splash moves up through all parts of the tree. Splash helps to feed the tree.

4. ______________________

Go on to the next page.

Name ______________________ Date ______________________

Assessment: Units 1, 2, 3 (p. 2)

Read the following paragraphs. Think about the underlined words. Read the paragraphs again with the new words given in the blanks. Fill in each second blank with a word that makes more sense.

Lisa is making a scrapbook with <u>rocks</u> she collects. The name of her scrapbook is "The Lions." The pictures are of the players on the Lions baseball team.

pencils

5. ______________________

Lisa is glad that she is <u>hearing</u> this scrapbook. She thinks it will help her remember how much fun playing baseball was.

finding

6. ______________________

Name ______________________ Date ______________________

Unit 1: Circle Clue Words

BENJAMIN FRANKLIN

Read the steps below.

Remember to do what good readers do:

1. *Read to make sense.*
2. *When a word doesn't make sense, think about what you already know.*
3. *Think about how the other words fit together to make sense.*
4. *Then, decide what the word should mean.*

Now read the following paragraphs. Then circle <u>two</u> words, or <u>groups</u> of words, that show the underlined word doesn't make sense in each paragraph.

Benjamin Franklin stopped going to school when he was only ten years old. He had to go to work. Benjamin still wanted to <u>sleep</u>, even if he was not in school. He learned many things just by reading. He was always reading.

Benjamin Franklin was always coming up with new ideas. One of his ideas was the Franklin stove. He made a stove that stood inside a <u>kite</u>. It made a room much hotter than a fireplace did. Even today, people use stoves that are very much like the stove that Franklin made.

Go on to the next page.

Name ______________________ Date ______________________

BENJAMIN FRANKLIN (P.2)

Read the following paragraphs. Circle two words, or groups of words, that show the underlined word doesn't make any sense in each paragraph.

As Franklin grew older, he found he needed glasses. He needed one pair of glasses to see things that were cold. He needed another pair of glasses to see things that were far away.

"I want to read books. I want to look at fire, water, and the stars. I want just one pair of shoes. I want just one pair so that I can see both near and far away," he said.

Benjamin Franklin made bifocals so that people needed only one pair of glasses to see both near and far away. The bifocals that animals wear today are very much like the ones Franklin made many years ago.

Name ______________________ Date ______________________

SEEING EYE DOGS

Read the following story. Circle <u>two</u> words, or <u>groups</u> of words, that show the underlined word doesn't make any sense in each paragraph.

Did you know that some dogs have <u>trunks</u>? These jobs are not working at a circus or doing tricks at home. Their jobs are to help people.

Some dogs help blind people. Other dogs help deaf people.

The dogs that help the blind are called Seeing Eye dogs. These dogs must go to special schools where they learn many <u>foods</u>. The person who wants the Seeing Eye dog must also go to the same school.

The school only picks special kinds of dogs. The dogs must like people and <u>laugh</u> well. They must sit, come, and stay when told.

Each Seeing Eye dog is fitted with a special bar. The dog learns to walk in front of the teacher and to cross streets. The <u>ball</u> must also learn not to play with other dogs when it is working.

Go on to the next page.

Name ______________________ Date ______________________

SEEING EYE DOGS (P.2)

Read the following story. Circle two words, or groups of words, that show the underlined word doesn't make any sense in each paragraph.

When the blind person comes to the school, he or she must learn how to take care of the dog. The blind person must also learn to tell the dog what to do. The person and the dog work never together. When they have learned to work with each other, the dog and its owner are ready to go home.

Dogs that are trained as hearing ear dogs listen very well and must be very smart.

At school, these dogs learn to follow hand signals. These hand signals are the "words" that the deaf people will use to tell a dog what to do. The dogs must learn to make for special sounds. When the doorbell rings, the dog must learn to pull the deaf person to the door. In the morning when the clock goes off, the hearing ear dog knows to wake up its owner.

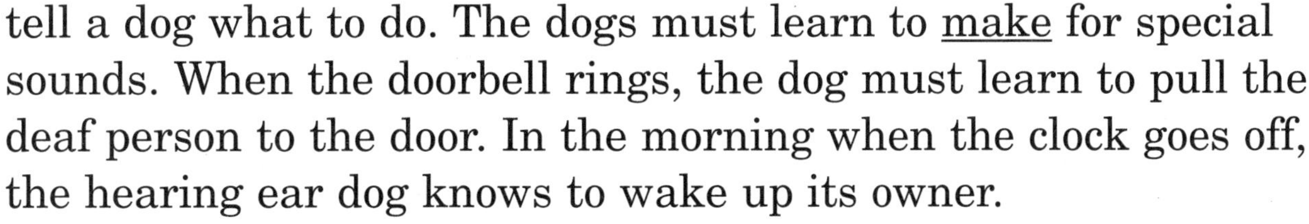

Many hearing ear dogs must also learn to tell parents if a baby is crying. A hearing ear dog learns to listen for many colors.

Seeing Eye and hearing ear dogs are very special. They work hard to help people. They are also loving pets.

  Cloze: Book A, SV 6182-6

Name ________________________ Date ________________________

Unit 2: Use What You Know

EATING CEREAL

Read the steps below.

Remember to do what good readers do:

1. *Read to make sense.*
2. *When a word doesn't make sense, read on to the end of the paragraph.*
3. *Think about what you already know.*
4. *Think about how the other words fit together to make sense.*
5. *Then, decide what the word should mean.*

Now read the following paragraph. Think about the underlined word. Fill in the blank with a word that makes more sense than the underlined word. Then REREAD the paragraph.

My mother calls me. She wants me to eat my cereal. It is made from whole wheat. My dad tells me the <u>house</u> helps the wheat grow. He says the sun helps plants and trees grow big and tall.

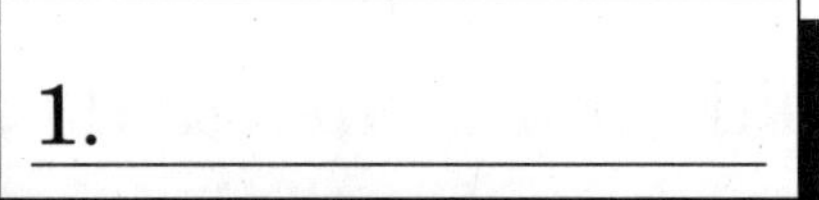

Name ______________________________ Date ______________________________

THE SUN

Read the following paragraphs. Think about the underlined words. Fill in each blank with a word that makes more sense. Then, read the paragraphs over to check the meaning.

While I am eating my cereal, I ask my parents a question: "How far away is the sun?" My mother tells me it is very far away from our planet, Earth. She says that the sun is a very big <u>bicycle</u>. It looks bigger than the other stars because it is nearer to Earth than other stars are.

1. ______________________

My dad says the sun keeps our planet warm. He says Earth would be dark and <u>hot</u> if there were no sun. Nothing could live without the sun.

2. ______________________

My dad also tells me that the sun will shine on the other side of our planet while I'm sleeping. He says that Earth <u>large</u> as it moves around the sun. It makes one full spin every day.

3. ______________________

When the side of the planet Earth we live on faces the sun, it is <u>slowly</u>. When our side is turned away from the sun, it is night.

4. ______________________

Name ______________________ Date ______________________

SPLASH

Read the following story. Think about the underlined words. Fill in each blank with a word that makes more sense. Then, read the story over to check the meaning.

This is the story of a raindrop. The raindrop's name is Splash.

Splash slides down the trunk of a tree. It <u>helps</u> on a little plant at the bottom of the tree. Splash slips down a leaf. It goes into a little pool made by many other raindrops.

1. ______________________

Splash sinks into the ground, under little roots, and slides around some rocks. Splash stops. It rests on one of the big tree <u>saws</u>. Then it is pulled inside the root. Pop! Slowly Splash goes up the root. Then Splash moves up through all parts of the tree. Splash helps to feed the tree.

2. ______________________

At the top of the tree, Splash turns into a gas and goes back to the clouds. In the <u>room</u>, Splash becomes a raindrop. Splash rests in a cloud for a while.

3. ______________________

Go on to the next page.

Name ______________________ Date ______________________

SPLASH (P.2)

Read the following story. Think about the underlined words. Fill in each blank with a word that makes more sense. Then, read the story over to check the meaning.

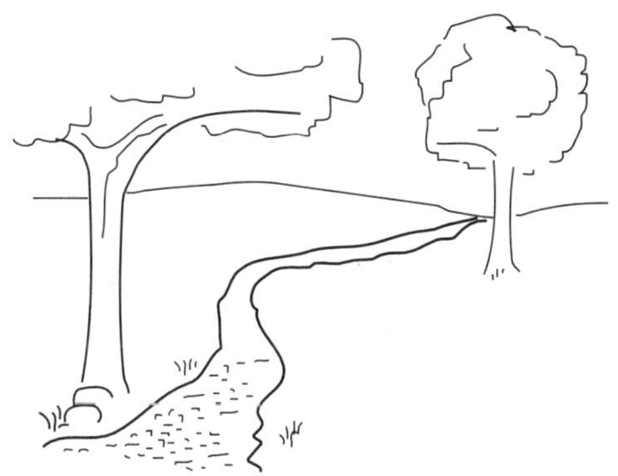

Other raindrops come up to the cloud, too. Soon there are lots of raindrops in the cloud.

This time the cloud goes over a mountain. It is very cold on top of the mountain. The water in the cloud freezes and turns into ice and snow. Now Splash becomes a very pretty <u>flower</u>. Splash and the other snowflakes fall on top of the mountain.

4. ______________________

The hot sun melts the snow. The melted snow and Splash then <u>fix</u> down the mountain. Splash and the melted snow turn into a little brook. The brook gets larger and larger and moves into a river.

5. ______________________

By now some of the other <u>rocks</u> in the river have turned back into a gas. They go up to the clouds while Splash is still having fun floating around in the big river.

6. ______________________

Name ______________________ Date ______________________

CATERPILLAR TO BUTTERFLY

Read the following story. Think about the underlined words. Fill in each blank with a word that makes more sense. Then, read the story over to check the meaning.

Some caterpillars <u>point</u> into butterflies. Other caterpillars turn into moths. This is surprising because caterpillars look very different from butterflies or moths. Let's see how caterpillars turn into butterflies. First, butterflies lay <u>bricks</u> on plants. The eggs are about as big as the head of a pin. Soon, caterpillars come out of the eggs. Little caterpillars look like tiny worms with many feet.

1. ______________________

2. ______________________

Some caterpillars have <u>happy</u> skin. Others have rough skin.

3. ______________________

As a butterfly caterpillar <u>sings</u>, it becomes too big to fit inside its skin. So the old skin cracks open and falls off. Now the caterpillar has a new, bigger skin. The caterpillar will get a new skin three or four times while it is growing.

4. ______________________

Go on to the next page.

Name ______________________ Date ______________________

CATERPILLAR TO BUTTERFLY (P.2)

Read the following story. Think about the underlined words. Fill in each blank with a word that makes more sense. Then, read the story over to check the meaning.

Butterfly <u>eggs</u> eat all day. Sometimes they eat all night, too. Caterpillars eat plants.

5. ______________________

Some butterfly caterpillars will grow as long as a <u>baseball</u>. Others will grow as big and fat as a crayon.

6. ______________________

After a few weeks, the butterfly caterpillar <u>reads</u> eating. It finds a plant to hold on to and spins a covering around itself. The covering is called a cocoon. The caterpillar inside the cocoon is now called a pupa.

7. ______________________

Inside the cocoon, the pupa is <u>drawing</u>. It is growing legs and wings and a whole new body, but you cannot see this happening. It is becoming a butterfly.

8. ______________________

Go on to the next page.

Name ______________________ Date ______________________

CATERPILLAR TO BUTTERFLY (P.3)

Read the following story. Think about the underlined words. Fill in each blank with a word that makes more sense. Then, read the story over to check the meaning.

One day the <u>window</u> cracks open. The butterfly pushes out its head. It sticks up its two feelers. Then it wiggles its body out of the cocoon. The new butterfly stands up on its six thin legs.

9. ______________________

The <u>wood</u> butterfly is wet. Its wings are folded. Now the butterfly pumps liquid into its wings. The liquid helps the butterfly to open them. Then the butterfly dries its wings by flapping them. You can see how different the butterfly looks from the caterpillar.

10. ______________________

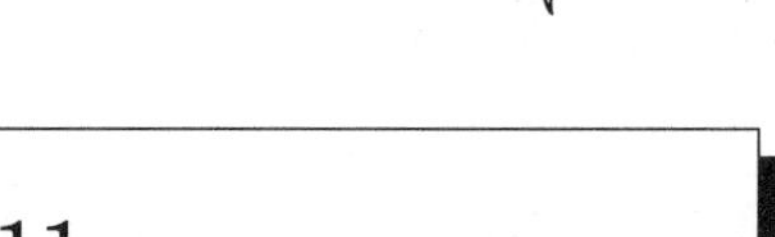

A butterfly lays <u>house</u>. A baby caterpillar comes out of each egg. The caterpillar spins a cocoon and turns into a pupa. Then the pupa turns into a butterfly. This is the caterpillar's wonderful surprise.

11. ______________________

Name ______________________ Date ______________________

FLYING KITES

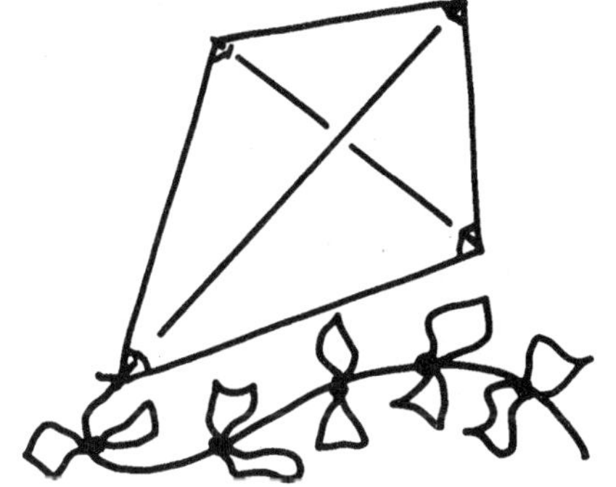

Read the following story. READ MORE before filling in the blanks. REREAD after you finish. Make any changes that help the whole story make sense.

Most kites have three main parts: a frame, a cover, and a flying line. The ① ____________ may be made of wood or plastic sticks. The cover is often made of paper, plastic, silk, or nylon. These materials are used because they are so light. Thin nylon string, which can be wrapped around a stick, is used for the flying line.

A tail is used to stop a kite from spinning on a windy ② ____________. The tails may be made of cloth, paper, or feathers. The larger a kite is, the bigger its tail needs to be.

There are hundreds of different kinds of kites, but most kites fit into one of five main groups. The first kind of kite is the flat kite. It is made of two crossed sticks, which are covered with material. It has a tail. A flat kite, like all kites, must be made so that the right and left ③ ____________ are exactly the same. If these sides are not exactly the same the kite will not fly.

The bow kite is the name of the second kind of kite. It is a short, wide kite that is shaped like a bow. Most bow kites do not have ④ ____________.

Go on to the next page.

Name ______________________ Date ______________________

FLYING KITES (P.2)

Read the following story. READ MORE before filling in the blanks. REREAD after you finish. Make any changes that help the whole story make sense.

The third kind of kite is the box kite. Box kites are shaped like a box. They are usually very large. Since box kites do not ⑤ ____________________ they do not need tails.

The fourth kind of kite, a flexi-kite, looks a paper airplane. Since a flexi-kite does not have a frame, it ⑥ __________________ and moves with the wind. Most flexi-kites do not have tails.

The last kind of kite, a novelty kite, may be made in many different shapes, ⑦ ____________________, or sizes. Chinese dragon kites, snake kites, and butterfly kites belong to this group. Bits of colored glass are sometimes tied to the kite's tail to make sounds as the kite flies.

Many famous people have flown kites. In 1752, Benjamin Franklin discovered electricity by flying a kite. The Wright brothers learned a lot about flying by watching box kites. This helped them to build their first airplane. Alexander Graham Bell, the inventor of the telephone, also made and flew kites. In 1907, he built a box kite that lifted a man 168 feet into the air! The man ⑧ ____________________ in the air for seven minutes.

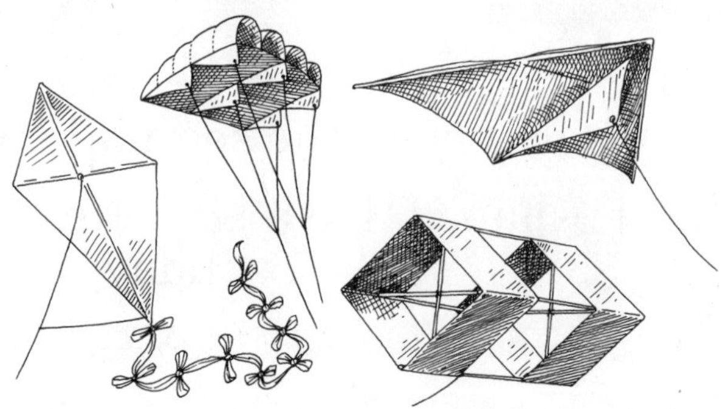

Name ______________________ Date ______________________

Unit 3: Read and Then Check

A SCRAPBOOK

Read the steps below.

Remember to do what good readers do:

1. *Read to make sense.*
2. *When a word doesn't make sense, READ MORE to the end of the paragraph.*
3. *Think about what you already know.*
4. *Think about how the other words fit together to make sense.*
5. *Decide what the word should mean.*
6. *Now, REREAD the paragraph to check the meaning of the new word.*

Read the following story. Think about the underlined words. Read the story again with the new words given in the blanks. Fill in each second blank with a word that makes more sense.

Terry is making a scrapbook about the <u>hard</u> party she had a few weeks ago. The name of her scrapbook is "My Favorite Birthday."

terrible

1. ______________

Terry has put many things into her scrapbook. There is a list of her <u>plants</u> who came to the party. There is a list of the games they played. There is a balloon Terry let the air out of when the party was over. There are also the birthday cards Terry got from her friends at the party.

toys

2. ______________

Name ______________________ Date ______________________

DOWN ON THE FARM

Read the following story. Think about the underlined words. Read the story again with the new words given in the blanks. Fill in each second blank with a word that makes more sense.

A farm is an interesting place to visit. Many animals dance on the farm. You'll see cows, pigs, chickens, and horses on the farm. You'll hear the sounds these animals make. You'll learn why farm animals are important.

draw
1. ______________

Before you get to the farm buildings, you can see the cows. They are standing behind a fence. Cows chew and chew with their mouths full. They brush flies away with their fingers.

glasses
2. ______________

The farmer raises some cows for meat. This coat is called beef.

sign
3. ______________

Go on to the next page.

Name ______________________ Date ______________________

DOWN ON THE FARM (P.2)

Read the following story. Think about the underlined words. Read the story again with the new words given in the blanks. Fill in each second blank with a word that makes more sense.

The farmer also raises some cows for milk. These cows are <u>dressed</u> in the barn. The farmer uses a machine to milk the cows. Maybe you can watch.

cooked

4. ______________________

Near the barn is the pig pen. There you might hear the <u>wishes</u> of the pigs. You can see the mother pig with her many babies. Baby pigs are called piglets. The farmer raises pigs for meat. This meat is called pork.

pieces

5. ______________________

The farmer's chickens may be inside the barn, or they may be running <u>during</u> the yard. Baby chickens are called chicks. You might hear the chickens clucking softly. Chickens give us eggs and meat.

since

6. ______________________

Name ______________________ Date ______________________

RUN, JUMP, THROW

Read the following story. Think about the underlined words. Read the story again with the new words given in the blanks. Fill each second blank with a word that makes more sense. Then, read the story again to check your new meaning.

What exercises do you do? Do you know that when you walk fast, run, swim, or ride your bike, you are really exercising? Do you know that when you cook rope or play tag you are also exercising?

tie
1. ______

Do you want to run faster? Would you like to jump tighter or throw a ball better? Here are some more exercises that are fun to do and good for you, too.

slower
2. ______

These exercises will help you move better and help make your body strong. Always find with stretching exercises to help you warm up. Numbers 1-4 are stretching exercises. Numbers 5-7 will help make your body strong.

talk
3. ______

1. Stand up. Bend down to touch your toes.

Go on to the next page.

Name ______________________________ Date ______________________________

RUN, JUMP, THROW (P.2)

Read the following story. Think about the underlined words. Read the story again with the new words given in the blanks. Fill each second blank with a word that makes more sense.

2. Sit with your <u>ears</u> out. Reach past your toes.

3. Sit with one leg out. Bend the other leg back. Reach out and try to touch your toes.

4. Stand with your feet flat on the floor. Lock your hands behind your <u>jail</u>. Turn slowly left, then right.

5. Stand with your feet flat on the floor. Then raise and lower your heels.

6. Lie on your back. Bend your knees. Keep your feet flat on the <u>airplane</u>. Lock your hands behind your head. Sit up and touch your elbows to your knees.

7. Pull yourself up on an exercise bar, or <u>sit</u> from it.

When you exercise, the last thing you should do is cool down. Give your body a chance to cool down slowly by doing some more stretching exercises.

books ______________________

4. ______________________

stomach ______________________

5. ______________________

roof ______________________

6. ______________________

hand ______________________

7. ______________________

Name ______________________________ Date ________________________________

Assessment: Units 4, 5, 6

Read the following paragraph. Think of a word that would make sense in the blank. Then, fill in the blank line.

Some people like to build things with dominoes. Then they like to watch them ① ____________________ down. If dominoes are set up in rows, they fall down in rows, too—one by one, faster and faster.

Read the following paragraphs. First, circle two words or groups of words that are clues for your thinking. Circle one <u>before</u> and one <u>after</u> the blank line. Then, fill in the blank line.

One side of each domino has nothing on it. The other side has two parts. The parts may have small white ② ____________________ on them, or they may be blank. The dots are called pips. This side is used for playing games.

The highest number of pips on one piece is 12. That piece has six pips on each part. A piece that has the same ③ ____________________ of pips on each part is called a double domino. This piece is the double six.

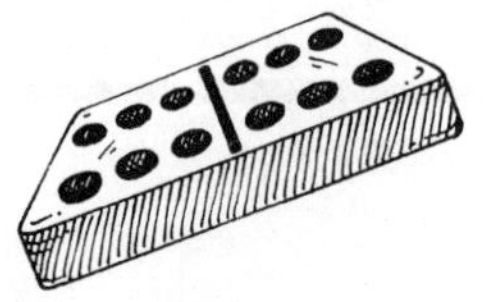

Go on to the next page.

Name ______________________ Date ______________________

Assessment: Units 4, 5, 6 (p. 2)

Read the following selection. Try each choice in the blank. Make sure only one choice makes sense. Circle the choice you think is correct.

Clouds are everywhere in the sky. Some are very high in the sky. Some float in the middle of the sky. Others are closer to the ④ ________________. The highest clouds are the coldest ones. These clouds are made of little bits of ice.

4. a) ground b) sky c) clouds

One good place to look for a cloud is on top of a mountain. Can you guess why you might find a cloud there? The answer is that air always grows colder as it moves up the side of a mountain. When the air reaches the ⑤ ________________ of the mountain, the water vapor has become little drops of water that form a cloud.

5. a) hat b) top c) snow

Name ______________________ Date ______________________

Unit 4: Read Beyond the Blank

DOMINOES

Read the following paragraphs. Think of a word that would make sense in the blank. Then, fill in the blank line.

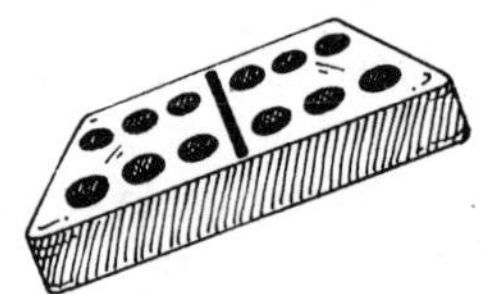

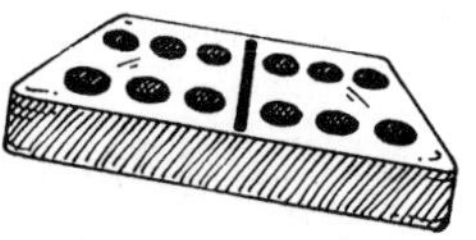

People have been playing with dominoes for a very long ① ____________________. No one knows just how old dominoes are, but they were used long, long ago in China.

Dominoes is a game. Have you played dominoes? Most dominoes are black with white spots on one ② ____________________. Sometimes the other side is plain. Many times the other side has a picture of a dragon.

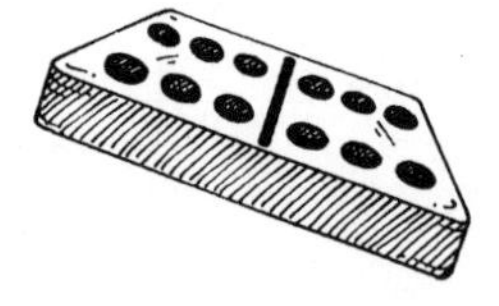

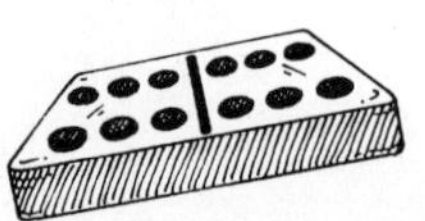

Go on to the next page.

Name ______________________ Date ______________________

DOMINOES (P.2)

Read the following paragraphs. Think of a word that would make sense in the blank. Then, fill in the blank line.

Some people like to build things with dominoes. Then they like to watch them fall down. If dominoes are set up in ③ __________________, they fall down in rows, too—one by one, faster and faster.

Many different games can be played with a set of dominoes. Most people play the block game. In this game the dominoes are placed on a ④ __________________ with the dotted side down. Each player takes five pieces. The rest of the dominoes are left in the pile on the table.

Each ⑤ __________________ tries to match one part of a domino to another. All the players try to be the first to play all their dominoes.

Name ______________________ Date ______________________

Unit 5: Circle Clue Words Before and After the Blank

SIX PIPS

Read the steps below.

Remember to do what good readers do:

1. Read to make sense.
2. When a word doesn't make sense, READ MORE to the end of the paragraph.
3. Think about what you already know.
4. Think about how the other words fit together to make sense.
5. Decide what the word should mean.
6. Now, REREAD to check the meaning of the whole paragraph.

Read the following paragraph. First, circle two words or groups of words that are clues for your thinking. Circle one before and one after the blank line. Then, fill in the blank line.

Most domino sets have 28 pieces. The pieces are almost always black and white. They are small and ① ______________. The pieces can stand on edge.

Go on to the next page.

Name ______________________ Date ______________________

SIX PIPS (P.2)

Read the following story. Circle <u>two</u> words or <u>groups</u> of words that help you think about the word that goes in the blank. Then, fill in the blank with a word that makes sense.

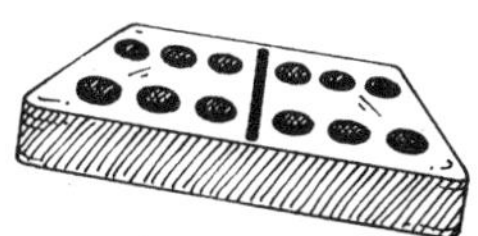

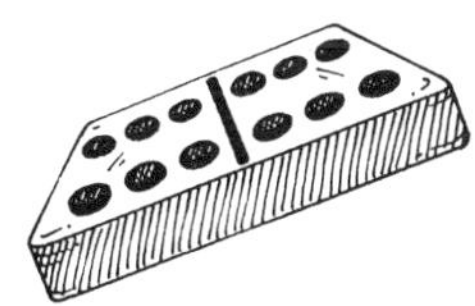

One side of each domino has nothing on it. The other side has two parts. The parts may have small white ② __________________ on them, or they may be blank. The dots are called pips. This side is used for playing games.

The highest number of pips on one piece is 12. That piece has six pips on each part.

A piece that has the same ③ __________________ of pips on each part is called a double domino. This piece is the double six.

The lowest number of pips on a domino is one. This piece has one pip on one part, and the ④ __________________ part is blank.

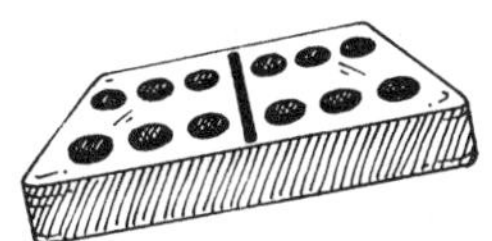

Name ______________________ Date ______________________

BLOCK GAME

Read the following story. Circle <u>two</u> words or <u>groups</u> of words that help you think about the word that goes in the blank. Then, fill in the blank with a word that makes sense.

Many different games can be played with a set of dominoes. Most people play the block game. In this game, the dominoes are ① ____________________ on a table with the pip side down. Each player takes five pieces. The rest of the dominoes are left in the pile on the table.

The player with the highest double domino goes first. That domino is put on the table pip side up. Suppose the first domino is the double three. The next player must ② ____________________ a domino that has three pips on one part. If the player does not have such a piece, then that player must pick from the pile of dominoes until a matching piece is found.

Suppose the second player plays the three-five piece. The third ③ ____________________ must use a piece with three or five pips.

As the game goes on, each player tries to match one part of a domino to another. All the players try to be the first to ④ ____________________ their pieces.

Name ______________________ Date ______________________

Unit 6: 3-Option Process of Elimination

LOOKING AT EARTH

Read the steps below.

Remember to do what good test-takers do:

1. *Read the story all the way through.*
2. *Read and think about each answer choice.*
3. *Ask yourself, "Does it sound right?"*
4. *Ask yourself, "Does it make sense with what I know?"*
5. *Ask yourself, "Does it make sense with all the clue words in the story?"*

Read the following paragraph. Try each choice in the blank. Make sure only one choice makes sense. Circle the choice you think is correct.

If you were up in space, you could see Earth floating like a big ball. If you came closer, you could see the clouds that __①__ Earth. If you came closer still, you could see that Earth is made of land and water.

1. a) make b) fly c) cover

Name ______________________ Date ______________________

WATER IN THE AIR

Read the following selection. Try each choice in the blank. Make sure only one choice makes sense. Circle the choice you think is correct.

The air is a wonderful collector. It collects bits of dust and smoke. Most of all, it collects water. As it moves over Earth, the air takes water from __①__ and lakes. It also takes water from plants and soil. Did you know that the air even collects water from you? Here is one way it happens.

1. a) moon b) pipes c) oceans

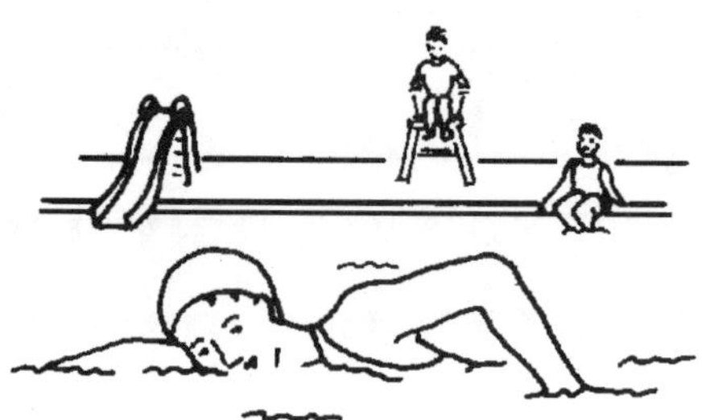

Suppose you are wet from swimming. You __②__ down to dry. As the sun dries you, it turns the water on your body into a gas called water vapor. The water vapor floats into the air, like tiny bubbles you can't see. As the bubbles float higher and higher, they grow colder and colder. When they become __③__ enough, the bits of vapor turn back into drops of water. Each drop forms around a tiny bit of dust. Many drops of water cling together to form a cloud.

2. a) sit b) swim c) wet
3. a) cold b) white c) growing

Name ______________________ Date ______________________

CLOUDS IN THE SKY

Read the following selection. Try each choice in the blank. Make sure only one choice makes sense. Circle the choice you think is correct.

Clouds are everywhere in the sky. Some are very high in the sky. Some __①__ in the middle of the sky. Others are closer to the ground. The highest clouds are the coldest ones. These clouds are made of little bits of ice.

1. a) pull b) float c) land

One good place to look for a cloud is on top of a mountain. Can you guess why you might find a cloud there? The answer is that air always grows colder as it moves up the side of a mountain. When the air __②__ the top of the mountain, the water vapor has become little drops of water that form a cloud.

2. a) grabs b) enters c) reaches

As the sun shines on this cloud, the cloud looks warm and bright. If you were to __③__ through a cloud, though, it would feel cold, dark, and very wet.

3. a) follow b) climb c) freezing

Name ______________________ Date ______________________

Clouds on the Ground

Read the following selections. Try each choice in the blank. Make sure only one choice makes sense. Circle the choice you think is correct.

Did you know that you could walk through a cloud without climbing a mountain? When you walk in fog, you are in a cloud that is on the __①__.

1. a) peak b) ground c) cold

When air is filled with water, it is called heavy air. Fog may form when heavy air near the ground cools. The water vapor in the air __②__ into big drops of water or ice. When the sun warms the air, the fog goes away.

2. a) turns b) drinks c) snows

Clouds and the Weather

Each kind of weather has its own kind of clouds. Some people read the clouds to __③__ what kind of weather is coming. How good are you at reading clouds? Do you know that white, puffy clouds high in the sky often mean good weather? Dark, puffy, flat-bottomed clouds low in the sky often mean rain.

3. a) story b) forget c) guess

Name ______________________ Date ______________________

Assessment: Units 7, 8, 9

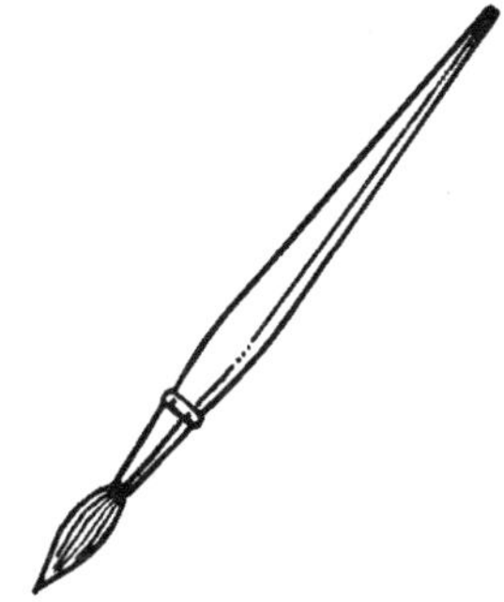

Read the following paragraphs. Try each choice in the blank. Make sure only one choice makes sense. Circle the choice you think is correct.

Henri Matisse was always trying new things. His art was different from that of other artists because of the way he used colors and __①__. Matisse said that when he wanted to paint a picture of fall, he did not try to copy just what he saw. Instead, he painted the way fall made him feel. Matisse never painted sad things, because he wanted his art to make people feel __②__.

1. a) food b) desks c) ships d) shapes e) dust
2. a) sad b) happy c) picture d) people e) cold

Read the following paragraph. Two clue words are underlined. The blank is a word that is <u>part of</u>, <u>a type of</u>, <u>typical of</u>, or <u>belongs to</u> the clue word. Circle the answer that makes the most sense. Then, fill in the sentence with the correct answer.

Tomie dePaola started to work on children's books by drawing the illustrations for them. He says, "As an <u>artist</u>, it is fairly easy to decide which stories I will do." He sometimes __③__ the <u>illustrations</u> for other authors' books, but he also writes and illustrates his own books.

3. a) draws b) stories c) writes d) laughs e) reads

______________________ is part of what an artist does to make illustrations.

Go on to the next page.

Name ______________________ Date ______________________

Assessment: Units 7, 8, 9 (p. 2)

Read the following selection. The blanks with the same number need the same word from the five choices. Use the whole selection. Use the words around all the blanks with the same number to help you pick your answer. Circle the answer choice for each number.

Claude Monet was born in France in 1840. He spent his early years in a __④__ where a great river ran into the sea. Claude loved the sea.

As a child, Claude was always sketching. People liked Claude's __⑤__. By working hard, Claude could sketch eight pictures a day and sell them.

By the time he was fifteen, Claude was already a famous artist in his home __④__. He sold his __⑤__ to a shop, which hung them in the window. The shop also showed the work of another artist.

4. a) room b) boat c) place d) country e) town
5. a) camera b) sketches c) drawing d) brushes e) colors

Name ______________________________ Date ________________________________

Unit 7: 5-Option Process of Elimination

A YOUNG ARTIST

Read the following paragraphs. Try each choice in the blank. Make sure only one choice makes sense. Circle the choice you think is correct.

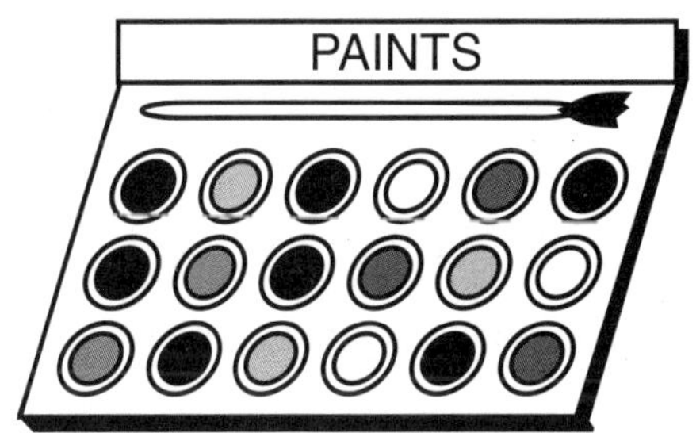

Henri Matisse was born in France in 1869. As a child, he didn't show any real interest in __①__. He studied law when he was a young man. Then one day, when he was sick, his mother brought him a box of paints to help him pass the time until he felt better.

1. a) law b) art c) games d) horses e) music

Matisse started to __②__ by making copies of famous paintings. He soon found that he liked to paint so much that he wanted to become an artist.

2. a) cry b) box c) paint d) ride e) draw

Name ______________________ Date ______________________

DRAWING WITH SCISSORS

Read the following selection. Try each choice in the blank. Make sure only one choice makes sense. Circle the choice you think is correct.

Matisse always kept trying new things. His art was very different from that of other artists because of the way he used __①__ and shapes. Matisse said that when he wanted to paint a picture of fall, he did not try to copy just what he saw. Instead, he painted the way fall made him feel. Matisse never painted __②__ things, because he wanted his art to make people feel happy.

1. a) food b) desks c) colors d) clocks e) dust
2. a) funny b) sad c) picture d) people e) warm

Matisse became a very famous artist. People began to buy more and more of his paintings.

When Matisse was over seventy years old, he __③__ using scissors and colored paper for his art. He cut out shapes and pasted these shapes on another piece of paper. Matisse called this "drawing with scissors."

3. a) started b) left c) hid d) quit e) never

Go on to the next page.

Name ______________________ Date ______________________

DRAWING WITH SCISSORS (P.2)

Read the following selection. Try each choice in the blank. Make sure only one choice makes sense. Circle the choice you think is correct.

In the last four years of his life, Matisse did only cutouts. He was not well, and this was the only work he could do. He didn't mind, though. When he was drawing with __④__, he said he was "cutting the colors out alive."

4. a) crayons b) paper c) country d) pens e) scissors

Matisse said that an artist has to look at life through the eyes of a child. By this he meant that an artist has to look at everything as if that artist were __⑤__ it for the first time.

5. a) losing b) washing c) planting d) seeing e) everything

To some people, Matisse's artwork might seem like the work of a child. In fact, it could only have been done by a great artist. Today Matisse's paintings and his cutouts are in __⑥__ all over the world.

6. a) drawing b) music c) boxes d) stories e) museums

Name ______________________ Date ______________________

GRAY SQUIRREL

Read the steps below.

Remember to do what good readers do:

1. *READ to make sense.*
2. *When something does not make sense, READ ON to the end of the paragraph.*
3. *THINK about what you already know.*
4. *THINK about what the other words tell you.*
5. *REREAD to check the sense of the whole paragraph with the possible word meaning.*
6. *READ MORE to check the sense of the whole story.*

Read the following paragraph. Think of the word that belongs in each blank. Write the word.

The gray squirrel is hungry. It comes down from its nest high up in a tree to look for food. As the squirrel runs along the ground, it sees a __①__. The __①__ looks very good, so the squirrel stops to have a bite to eat. The squirrel turns the __①__ in its paws as it takes small bites. A __①__ isn't what the squirrel really wants, though.

Name ______________________________ Date ______________________________

FLOATING

Read the following paragraph. Think of a word that would make sense in each blank. Write the word.

It was a sunny morning on the river. Thewater slapped softly at a __①__ moving through the water. A man was rowing the __①__, but he was not a fisherman on his way out to catch fish. He was an artist on his way out to paint a landscape. The __①__ was his floating studio, or working place.

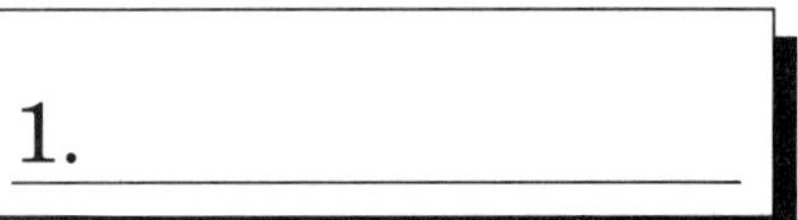

Name ______________________ Date ______________________

FAMOUS AT FIFTEEN

Read the following story. The blanks with the same number need the same word from the five choices. Use the whole story. Use the words around all the blanks with the same number to help you pick your answer. Circle the answer choice for each number.

Claude Monet was born in France in 1840. He spent his early years in a __①__ where a __⑧__ river ran into the sea. Claude loved the sea.

As a child, Claude was always sketching. People liked Claude's __②__. By working hard, Claude could sketch eight pictures a day and sell them.

By the time he was fifteen, Claude was already a famous artist in his home __①__. He sold his __②__ to a __③__, which hung them in the window. The __③__ also showed the work of another artist, named Mr. Boudin.

1. a) boat
   b) room
   c) town
   d) country
   e) place

2. a) colors
   b) brushes
   c) drawing
   d) sketches
   e) camera

3. a) person
   b) shop
   c) artist
   d) sea
   e) park

Go on to the next page.

Name ______________________________ Date ______________________________

FAMOUS AT FIFTEEN (P.2)

Read the following story. The blanks with the same number need the same word from the five choices. Use the whole story. Use the words around all the blanks with the same number to help you pick your answer. Circle the answer choice for each number.

One day the two artists met at the __③__. Mr. Boudin said to Claude, "So, young man, it's you who does these little __②__. They have something in them, but why not try painting? I will be happy to give you __④__."

At first Claude had no answer. He didn't like Mr. Boudin's paintings. He wasn't sure that he __⑤__ Mr. Boudin to teach him to __⑥__. Finally, Claude agreed.

Mr. Boudin __⑦__ Claude how to __⑥__ sunlight and shadows. He __⑦__ Claude a __⑧__ deal about painting. When the __④__ ended, Claude knew that he __⑤__ to be a painter for the rest of his life. At the age of seventeen, Claude went to the city of Paris to study more about art.

4. a) away
   b) paintings
   c) money
   d) lessons
   e) time

5. a) wanted
   b) felt
   c) told
   d) agreed
   e) painted

6. a) paint
   b) find
   c) see
   d) make
   e) sell

7. a) found
   b) watched
   c) left
   d) knew
   e) taught

8. a) some
   b) great
   c) small
   d) wide
   c) fast

Name ______________________ Date ______________________

Unit 9: Form Categories

WHITEBIRD

Read the following story. One or two clue words are underlined in each paragraph. The blank is a word that is <u>part of</u>, a <u>type of</u>, <u>typical of</u>, or <u>belongs to</u> the clue words. Circle the answer that makes the most sense. Then, fill in the sentence with the correct answer.

The only way to get to Tomie dePaola's house is to go down a winding <u>country</u> road, past a lake and many maple trees. Tomie lives in a __①__ called Whitebird, tucked into a small New England village.

What was once a barn is now dePaola's studio. On the <u>wall</u> of his studio __②__ a pink <u>banner</u> with paper cutouts of some of his characters. Some children in Minnesota gave him this banner. The children shaped the "o" in Tomie like a heart because dePaola often uses hearts in his pictures.

Tomie dePaola started to work on children's books by drawing the illustrations for them. He says, "As an <u>artist</u>, it is fairly easy to decide which stories I will do." He sometimes __③__ the <u>illustrations</u> for other authors' books, but he also writes and illustrates his own books.

1. a) field
   b) apartment
   c) hotel
   d) hut
   e) farmhouse

A ______________ is part of the country.

2. a) lies
   b) plants
   c) hangs
   d) draws
   e) sits

______________ is typical of a banner on a wall.

3. a) writes
   b) laughs
   c) reads
   d) draws
   e) stories

______________ is part of what an artist does to make illustrations.

Name ______________________ Date ______________________

STORY CHARACTERS

Read the following story. One or two clue words are underlined in each paragraph. The blank is a word that is <u>part of</u>, a <u>type of</u>, <u>typical of</u>, or <u>belongs to</u> the clue words. Circle the answer that makes the most sense. Then, fill in the sentence with the correct answer.

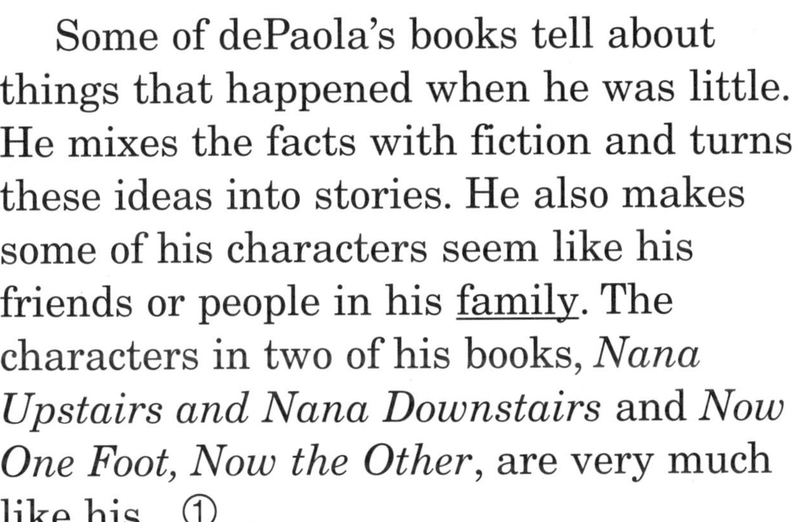

Some of dePaola's books tell about things that happened when he was little. He mixes the facts with fiction and turns these ideas into stories. He also makes some of his characters seem like his friends or people in his <u>family</u>. The characters in two of his books, *Nana Upstairs and Nana Downstairs* and *Now One Foot, Now the Other*, are very much like his __①__.

Tomie dePaola loves children. He says, "I don't think of children as being children. When I find myself in the company of <u>children</u>, I never realize that we're different ages. They're just __②__!" Then that special laugh spills out.

Tomie dePaola __③__ with hundreds of children when he is on a <u>trip</u>. He likes to know what they are thinking. He feels it is important for children to <u>meet</u> the authors of the books they like to read. He thinks that "it makes the books come alive for them."

1. a) dogs
   b) houses
   c) pictures
   d) pets
   e) grandparents

   ______________ belong to a family.

2. a) older
   b) slower
   c) taller
   d) shorter
   e) wider

   ______________ is typical of children.

3. a) sends
   b) talks
   c) rides
   d) calls
   e) drifts

   ______________ is part of meeting people on a trip.

Name ______________________ Date ______________________

A Patchwork Quilt

Read the following story. The blank is an answer choice that is <u>part of</u>, a <u>type of</u>, <u>typical of</u>, or <u>belongs to</u> another clue word in the story. The clue word is not underlined. First circle your answer choice. Then, circle the clue word in the story that the answer is <u>part of</u>.

Long ago, it was unusual for old clothes to be thrown away. The parents' old clothes were made smaller to fit their children. Any extra pieces of __①__ went into the scrap bag. When the bag was full, it was time to make a patchwork quilt.

At first, these scraps did not look much like a quilt. They were just pieces of cloth in many colors and sizes. Making all of these scraps look as if they belonged together was one of the jobs of the patchwork quilt maker. The other job was then to __②__ the quilt together, using a fancy design.

People who made quilts were like artists without brushes or paint. Tiny bits of cloth and fancy stitches became beautiful designs. The ideas for these quilt designs came from everyday life. One pattern called "Log Cabin" came from the way the __③__ in a cabin wall looked. Another one, called "Sunshine and Shadow," looked like plowed fields.

1. a) metal
   b) glass
   c) cloth
   d) ink
   e) food

2. a) stitch
   b) melt
   c) cook
   d) find
   e) tear

3. a) well
   b) logs
   c) table
   d) floor
   e) field

Go on to the next page.

Name ______________________ Date ______________________

A PATCHWORK QUILT (P.2)

Read the following story. The blank is an answer choice that is <u>part of</u>, a <u>type of</u>, <u>typical of</u>, or <u>belongs to</u> another clue word in the story. The clue word is not underlined. First circle your answer choice. Then, circle the clue word in the story that the answer is <u>part of</u>.

Children were taught to quilt as soon as they could hold a needle. Older children sometimes made a quilt to welcome a new __④__ into a family. These quilts were passed down from family to family.

A quilt is made the same way a sandwich is made. Cloth is used for the top and bottom layers just like __⑤__. Long ago, old cotton, wool, straw, cornhusks, and even old letters were used as stuffing for the quilt.

It took a long time to make a patchwork quilt. Usually, only the top of the __⑥__ was made from the scraps of cloth. Sometimes scraps of cloth were used for both the top and the bottom layers. When it was time for the quilt to be stuffed and stitched together, a quilting bee was often held.

The quilters sat around the frame to work on the quilt. They sewed three of the edges of the top and __⑦__ layers together. Next the quilt was stuffed. Then the three layers were sewn together with tiny stitches.

4. a) baby
   b) quilt
   c) tree
   d) cabin
   e) lesson

5. a) ketchup
   b) scraps
   c) bread
   d) meat
   e) paper

6. a) paint
   b) needle
   c) cloth
   d) design
   e) quilt

7. a) frame
   b) stuffed
   c) scraps
   d) bottom
   e) both

Name ______________________ Date ______________________

Assessment: Units 10, 11

Read the following story. The underlined clue word causes, or makes, or results from the word that goes in the blank. Circle the answer that makes the most sense. Then, fill in the sentence with the most meaningful answer.

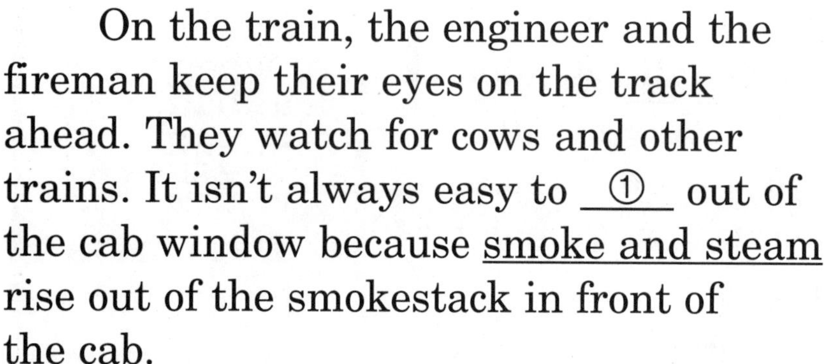

On the train, the engineer and the fireman keep their eyes on the track ahead. They watch for cows and other trains. It isn't always easy to ____①____ out of the cab window because smoke and steam rise out of the smokestack in front of the cab.

The engineer uses a wooden hand brake to stop the train. Each car has its own hand brake, which is on top of the car. The engineer has to signal the other crew members in order to bring the whole train to a ____②____.

1. a) jump
   b) see
   c) yell
   d) leave
   e) rise

Smoke and steam make it hard to ________ something ahead.

2. a) start
   b) stop
   c) pull
   d) hand
   e) hill

Hand brakes cause the train to

____________.

Go on to the next page.

Name ______________________ Date ______________________

Assessment: Units 10,11 (p.2)

Read the following selection. Circle the choice you think is correct.

A worker is digging ___③___ the Pottery Shop. When a visitor asks her what she is doing, the worker says that she is digging for clay. The clay is used to make plates, bowls, and cups. Each step in making them takes place in this shop.

The sound of a worker's ___④___ as it hits iron can be heard everywhere in this part of the village. An excited group crowds around the Blacksmith Shop and watches thc flashes of fire as the blacksmith pounds new farm tools into shape. The village farmers also bring all their ___⑤___ farm tools to the Blacksmith Shop to be fixed.

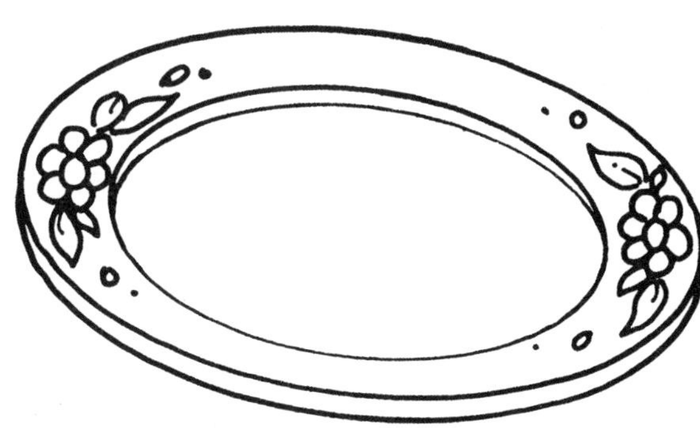

3. a) after
   b) when
   c) slowly
   d) outside
   e) on

4. a) anvil
   b) hammer
   c) foot
   d) hand
   e) shovel

5. a) earth
   b) cool
   c) new
   d) painted
   e) broken

Name ______________________ Date ______________________

STEAM ENGINE

Read the following paragraph. The underlined clue word <u>causes</u>, or <u>makes</u>, or <u>results from</u> the word that goes in the blank. Circle the answer that makes the most sense. Then, fill in the sentence with the most meaningful answer.

Long ago, trains were pulled by steam-engine locomotives. A steam engine burned coal to heat water. A car, or tender, filled with coal and water was right behind the locomotive. A __①__ heated the water in a boiler and <u>steam was formed</u>. The steam pushed the parts connected to the wheels and that made the locomotive move.

1. a) caboose
   b) train
   c) shovel
   d) fire
   e) pan

______________________ causes water to turn to steam.

Go on to the next page.

Name ______________________ Date ______________________

STEAM ENGINE (P.2)

Read the following paragraph. The underlined clue word causes, or makes, or results from the word that goes in the blank. Circle the answer that makes the most sense. Then, fill in the sentence with the most meaningful answer.

The engineer and the fireman rode in the cab of the locomotive. The engineer ran the train. The fireman's job was to keep the fire burning in the firebox. This was done by throwing __②__ into the firebox.

The engineer and the fireman also kept their eyes on the track ahead. They watched for cows and other trains. It wasn't always easy to __③__ out of the cab window because smoke and steam rose out of the smokestack in front of the cab.

The engineer used a wooden hand brake to stop the train. Each car had its own hand brake, which was on top of the car. The engineer had to signal the other crew members in order to bring the whole train to a __④__.

2. a) water
   b) food
   c) freight
   d) coal
   e) passengers

______________ causes a fire to burn.

3. a) yell
   b) see
   c) leave
   d) rise
   e) jump

Smoke and steam make it hard to ________ something ahead.

4. a) stop
   b) start
   c) hand
   d) pull
   e) hill

Hand brakes caused the train to ____________.

Cloze: Book A, SV 6182-6

Name ______________________ Date ______________________

THE EDGE OF WATER

Read the following story. The blank in the story is an answer choice that causes, makes, or results from another clue word in the story. The clue word is not underlined. First circle your answer choice. Then, circle the clue word in the story that the answer results from or causes.

A beach, or shore, is the land along the edge of a body of water. The __①__ on a beach was once large rocks and seashells that over a period of many, many years were pounded down by the wind and the water into very tiny bits or grains.

A beach is the home of a great number of living things. High tide, or the rise of the tide, is when the water moves up onto the beach in waves. As the __②__ moves along the shore, it carries living and nonliving things with it. After some time, the tide begins to fall and the water moves back down to a lower level, or low tide. During the fall of tides, many living and nonliving things are __③__ on the beach. This happens twice each day.

1. a) waves
   b) people
   c) sand
   d) birds
   e) fish

2. a) water
   b) beach
   c) whale
   d) light
   e) sand

3. a) singing
   b) donc
   c) tried
   d) dried
   e) left

Name ____________________________ Date ______________________________

STORM AT THE BEACH

Read the following story. The blank in the story is an answer choice that causes, makes, or results from another clue word in the story. The clue word is not underlined. First circle your answer choice. Then, circle the clue word in the story that the answer results from or causes.

A storm is also a time when living and nonliving things are ___①___ up by the current and left along the beach. Some of the living things left on the beach are animals such as crabs, shellfish, and starfish. Seaweed and other plants can also be found. Some of the nonliving things that can be found on the beach are empty shells, rocks, and driftwood.

The beach is also ___②___ for plants, as well as sand and sea animals. These living things are able to live together, take care of one another, and respect each other. Each animal or plant fits into a special place in its home and touches the life of every other thing that lives around it. Empty shells, rocks, and driftwood act to ___③___ the plants, the sand animals, and the sea animals from things that might harm or even kill them.

1. a) thought
   b) left
   c) flying
   d) pulled
   e) looked

2. a) tide
   b) home
   c) sea
   d) wave
   e) shell

3. a) protect
   b) lose
   c) track
   d) kill
   e) find

Name ______________________________ Date ______________________________

SANDY BEACH FUN

Read the following story. The blank in the story is an answer choice that <u>causes</u>, <u>makes</u>, or <u>results from</u> another clue word in the story. The clue word is not underlined. First circle your answer choice. Then, circle the clue word in the story that the answer <u>results from</u> or <u>causes</u>.

Did you ever move a rock or pick up a shell and discover the home of a small sea animal? A hermit crab will often find the empty shell of another sea animal and use it for a home. Inside the __①__, the hermit crab will be safe from strong winds, rough currents, other animals, and even people.

The beach is a place you can enjoy with all your senses. Use your sense of touch as you walk along the edge of the water and feel the sand under your __②__ feet and between your toes. You can almost taste the salt from the water, and you can smell the fresh sea air. Hear the sound of the waves __③__ against the shore. Watch carefully for animals that live in the sand and water. Life and color and unusual shapes are on a sandy beach waiting for you to explore them.

1. a) waves
   b) shell
   c) danger
   d) wind
   e) rock

2. a) new
   b) empty
   c) bare
   d) covered
   e) long

3. a) curling
   b) laughing
   c) burning
   d) covering
   e) slapping

Name ______________________ Date ______________________

LIVING HISTORY MUSEUM

Read the steps below.

Remember to do what good test-takers do:

1. *Read the story all the way through.*
2. *REREAD and think about each answer choice.*
3. *Ask yourself, "Does it sound right?"*
4. *Ask yourself, "Does it make sense with what I know?"*
5. *Ask yourself, "Does it make sense with the whole paragraph and story?"*
6. *READ MORE to help eliminate choices when you cannot pick one.*

Read the following selection. Circle the choice you think is correct.

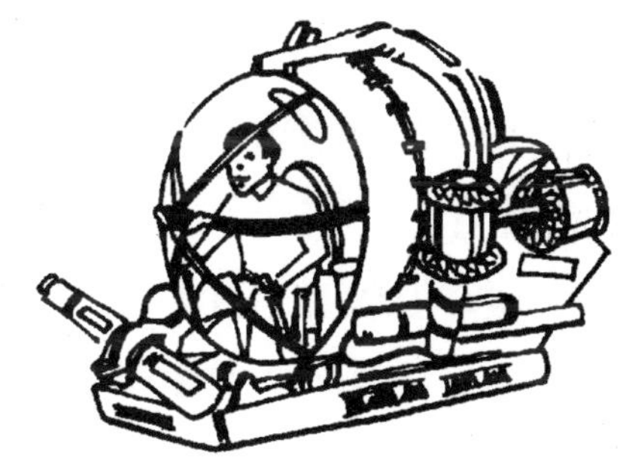

A ride on a time machine back to the days when the United States was a new country would be exciting. __①__ Old Sturbridge Village in Massachusetts is like taking a time-machine ride. Old Sturbridge Village is known as a living history museum. A living history museum is a museum that shows life as it used to be at a particular time and place in the __②__. Sturbridge Village is a good place to learn about country village life in early America.

1. a) Writing
   b) Leaving
   c) Visiting
   d) Drawing
   e) Making

2. a) water
   b) past
   c) future
   d) life
   e) present

Name ______________________ Date ______________________

THE CENTER VILLAGE

Read the following selection. Circle the choice you think is correct.

Old Sturbridge Village was opened to visitors in 1946. Old Sturbridge Village is divided into sections: Center Village, Seasonal Exhibits, the Countryside, and the Mill Neighborhood. The Center Village is made up of houses, meeting houses, the Printing Office, and a bank. The Countryside is made up of the District School, a Pottery Shop, and farms. More than forty __①__ of the kind that were built from 1790 to 1840 were brought in from places around New England. They were then __②__ onto the village land and put in working order.

At the village about four hundred people now live and work the same way that the people did who lived and worked in this part of America long ago. The people who live there today even dress as the people of __③__ America dressed.

1. a) people
   b) banks
   c) sections
   d) buildings
   e) bricks

2. a) built
   b) moved
   c) found
   d) sold
   e) farmed

3. a) South
   b) modern
   c) western
   d) middle
   e) early

Name ______________________ Date ______________________

VISIT OLD STURBRIDGE VILLAGE

Read the following selections.
Circle the choice you think is correct.

1. a) book
   b) press
   c) shop
   d) rail
   e) print

2. a) build
   b) attend
   c) draw
   d) miss
   e) pass

3. a) clothes
   b) dances
   c) alphabet
   d) songs
   e) benches

A visit to the Printing Shop would show workers setting books by hand just as printers of early America did. A press bangs slowly as pages of the __①__ are printed. A rail is connected to the ceiling. The pages hang on the rail ready to dry. Some visitors say that the drying pages remind them of wash that is drying on a clothesline.

When children from other places visit Old Sturbridge Village, these children become part of the village. They __②__ the District School in the Countryside, which has only one room and one teacher. The children sit on wooden benches and share long wooden desks. They learn how to read, write, and count. Children practice their __③__ on small black slates. Girls wear bonnets and long dresses, and the boys wear shirts and trousers.

Name ______________________ Date ______________________

WORKERS IN THE VILLAGE

Read the following selection. Circle the choice you think is correct.

A worker is digging __①__ the Pottery Shop. When a visitor asks him what he is doing, the worker says that he is digging for clay. The clay is used to make plates, bowls, and cups. Each step in making them takes place in this shop.

Bang! Bang! Bang! The sound of a worker's __②__ as it hits iron can be heard everywhere in this part of the village. An excited group crowds around the Blacksmith Shop and watches the flashes of fire as the blacksmith pounds new farm tools into shape. The village farmers also bring all their __③__ farm tools to the Blacksmith Shop to be fixed.

At the Freeman Farm, the village farmers can be seen plowing fields and growing crops which are used as food for the villagers. Farm animals are as important as the field crops. These farm __④__ provide food, power, transportation, and wool for clothing.

1. a) after
   b) slowly
   c) outside
   d) on
   e) when

2. a) foot
   b) anvil
   c) shovel
   d) hammer
   e) hand

3. a) new
   b) painted
   c) broken
   d) cool
   e) earth

4. a) crops
   b) fields
   c) food
   d) villages
   e) animals

ANSWER KEY

Units 1, 2, 3 Assessment,

p. 8-9
Possible answers:
1. dogs, 2. schools, 3. lands, 4. roots, 5. pictures, 6. making

Unit 1: Circle Clue Words

p. 10, 11
Possible answers:
work, reading
stove, stood inside
glasses, see
read books, look, see both near and far
people, see both near and far

p. 12, 13
Possible answers:
dogs, jobs
schools, learn
sit, come, stay
learn, play, dogs
learn to tell, with each other
listen, to, for, doorbell rings
hearing ear, listen

Unit 2: Use What You Know

p. 14
1. sun

p. 15
Possible answers:
1. star
2. cold
3. spins
4. day

p. 16-17
Possible answers:
1. lands
2. roots
3. cloud
4. snowflake
5. roll
6. raindrops

p. 18-20
Possible answers:
1. turn
2. eggs
3. smooth
4. grows
5. caterpillars
6. finger, nail, pencil
7. finishes, stops
8. growing
9. cocoon
10. new
11. eggs

p. 21-22
Possible answers:
1. frame
2. day
3. sides
4. tails
5. spin
6. bends
7. colors
8. stayed

Unit 3: Read and Then Check

p. 23
Possible answers:
1. birthday
2. friends

p. 24-25
Possible answers:
1. live
2. tails
3. meat
4. milked
5. sounds
6. around

p. 26-27
Possible answers:
1. jump
2. higher
3. begin/start
4. legs
5. head
6. floor
7. hang

Units 4, 5, 6 Assessment,

p. 28-29
Possible answers:
1. fall
2. circle "small white," "dots"
dots
3. circle "six," "pips"
number
4. a
5. b

Unit 4: Read Beyond the Blank

p. 30-31
Possible answers:
1. time
2. side
3. rows
4. table
5. player

Unit 5: Circle Clue Words Before and After the Blank

p. 32-33
Possible answers:
1. circle "small and," "on edge"
square/flat/narrow
2. circle "white," "dots"
dots
3. circle "number," "of pips"
number
4. circle "one part," "blank"
other

p. 34
Possible answers:
1. circle "a table," "the pile"
placed
2. circle "goes first," "put on the table," "must pick"
use/play
3. circle "second player," "third"
player
4. circle "all the players," "the first," "their pieces"
use

Unit 6: 3-Option Process of Elimination

p. 35
1. c

p. 36
1. c
2. a
3. a

p. 37
1. b
2. c
3. b

p. 38
1. b
2. a
3. c

Units 7, 8, 9 Assessment,

p. 39-40
1. d
2. b
3. a, Drawing
4. e
5. b

Unit 7: 5-Option Process of Elimination

p. 41
1. b
2. c

p. 42-43
1. c
2. b
3. a
4. e
5. d
6. e

Unit 8: Use Redundant Clues

p. 44
Possible answer:
1. flower (not nut)

p. 45
Possible answer:
1. raft or boat

p. 46-47
1. c
2. d
3. b
4. d
5. a
6. a
7. e
8. b

Unit 9: Form Categories

p. 48
1. e, farm
2. c, Hanging
3. d, Drawing

p. 49
1. e, Grandparents
2. d, Being short
3. b, Talking

p. 50-51
Circle words may vary.
1. c, clothes/scrap/quilt
2. a, jobs/quilt
3. b, cabin walls
4. a, children/family
5. c, sandwich/top and bottom layers
6. e, make/top/scraps
7. d, sewed/edges/top

Units 10, 11 Assessment,

p. 52-53
1. b, see
2. b, stop
3. d
4. b
5. e

Unit 10: Find Causes and Effects

p. 54-55
1. d, Fire
2. d, Coal
3. b, see
4. a, stop

p. 56
Circled answers may vary.
1. c, beach/large rocks/seashells/pounded down
2. a, tide/waves/shore
3. e, fall of tides

p. 57
Circled answers may vary.
1. d, storm/current
2. b, beach/live together
3. a, empty shells/rocks/driftwood/harm/kill

p. 58
Circled answers may vary.
1. b, home/hermit crab
2. c, feel the sand/feet/between your toes
3. e, hear the sound/waves/against the shore

Unit 11: Process of Elimination

p. 59
1. c
2. b

p. 60
1. d
2. b
3. e

p. 61
1. a
2. b
3. c

p. 62
1. c
2. d
3. c
4. e